The really useful OWL GUIDE

Jemima Parry-Jones

CONTENTS

Introduction

When I was asked if I would like to write this guide, I have to say that I was not too happy about the idea, mainly because I don't think that owls make particularly good pets. They are more complicated to look after than other, more commonly understood pets and, if they are to be flown, it is very easy to make a mistake and kill them.

Added to that, in my experience children often lose interest in owning an animal or bird and then the poor parent is landed with the task of caring for it, which is hard on both the parent and the owl.

I was concerned that, by writing this book, I might be encouraging people to own owls, when actually they are quite specialist pets and need knowledge and understanding to be cared for properly. They also take up a considerable amount of time. However, many people already have owls and have been given either poor or no advice on how to look after them. So, hopefully, this book will give you the basics on how to care for an owl, buying, housing, feeding, living with one and a little on the training.

That said, I have still not changed my opinion on children having an owl as a pet without first proving their interest over an extended period. Also, you must remember that if you do look after an owl, depending on the species, it can live twice as long as the average dog and be with you longer than the children!

Chapter 1 Understanding an owl

The different types

There are about 130 species of owl, ranging from the tiniest Elf Owl at under 100g (3.5oz) to the largest Eurasian Eagle Owl weighing in at up to 4kg (9lb). Neither is suitable for a child to keep! Owls are divided into two main groups. Eleven species make up one group; the Barn Owls, and two species called Bay Owls belong to this group. The rest of the other 120 or so are in a second group, sometimes called the Eared Owls. By this I do not mean real ears, like yours and mine, although obviously owls do have ears. This name refers to the feather ear tufts that look like ears. Just to make matters more difficult, not all the owls in this group have feather ear tufts although they belong to the Eared Owl group. It is all very complicated; even the scientists don't agree but, if you are interested in learning more about this side of things, you will find a list of books to read at the back of this book.

Left to right: Snowy Owl, Great Grey Owl, Barn Owl, Eagle Owl, and Little Owl.

In Britain, six species of owl live in the wild, although the Snowy Owl is found only in the very north of Scotland and then only rarely. Our commonest wild owl is the Tawny Owl, and it is thought that about 100,000 pairs live in the United Kingdom. The Barn Owl is not doing very well in the wild, mainly through changes in habitat and also the increased number of cars on the roads. The Little Owl is what is called an 'introduced' species or, even more technically, a 'non indigenous' species. This means that it did not originate from, in this case, the United Kingdom but instead was brought in from another country and released here. The Little Owl was brought into the south-east of England in the latter part of the 18th century and, considering no more than 35 birds were released, they have done pretty well as there are about 8,000 pairs to date. They come from – are indigenous to – southern Europe and if you look at their scientific name, *Athene noctua*, you can guess that they are found in Greece. The other two species are the Long-eared Owl and the Short-eared Owl, neither of which are particularly common.

All the owls tend to stand quite upright, indeed they are capable of looking like two quite different birds. They can stand up really tall and thin with their huge eyes half shut, or they can look like a big round ball with their great, forward-facing eyes wide open. It is these eyes and the beak half-hidden in the feathers on its face that make it look somewhat human, and this is one of the reasons why the owl is so popular.

Same owl, different posture.

The feather colour of the owls is quite beautiful. Muted soft colours help them to blend in with their surroundings and serve as camouflage. This is important because owls are not liked by other birds and can be attacked and mobbed during daylight hours. They can have either yellow, orange or brown eyes; it is thought that the darker the eye colour the more nocturnal the species of owl. Therefore, the Snowy Owl and the Burrowing Owl, both of which are diurnal (come out in the daylight), have yellow eyes. The Eagle Owls tend to have orange eyes and are what is called crepuscular – they like to hunt in the half light at dawn and dusk. The Barn Owl, with its dark brown eyes, is rather more nocturnal.

You must remember one important thing. During the breeding season, all the owls will hunt whenever they can, to feed their young. They cannot afford to wait for the short hours of darkness in the late spring and summer to feed hungry, calling babies who are telling them that it's time to get up. At this time of year, they hunt more in daylight than in the dark.

Most of the owls look much larger than they really are. The soft, loose feathers cover what is a surprisingly small body, especially with the birds that come from the colder areas of the world. The Great Grey Owl, for example, looks as large as the Eurasian Eagle Owl but is less than half its weight.

How they live
In the wild, many owls tend to be solitary birds, only living in pairs during the breeding season when they have eggs and young to tend. A few species will group together in winter, but this is unusual. Mostly owls hide away on their own, in a hollow or crevice, up against the trunk of a tree or hidden in ivy, coming out at night, dawn or dusk to hunt and

live. Therefore, a trained working owl does not usually mind being kept alone as this would be fairly normal for it anyway, except during the breeding season. Most of the owls are nocturnal, which means that during the day they don't do a great deal. This is one of the things to be remembered by those of you who are considering keeping an owl.

Visit some of the Owl or Bird of Prey Centres around the country. Look at the owls and see what they do in their aviary during the day – and you will find it's not a lot. In fact, unless they are down to flying weight and haven't been flown yet that day, even the trained owls often hide in their boxes or at the back of the pens for most of the day.

Where they live

Owls live in all sorts of different habitats, from huge rain forests to the edges of deserts, on farmland, moorland, marshlands, in woods and on plains. Also they have adapted to live in very different climates. The Snowy Owl and the Hawk Owl can cope with very cold weather and, in fact, don't like very hot temperatures, but they do not deal well with wet conditions as normally it does not rain very much in the Arctic. Some of our owls at The National Birds of Prey Centre, for example, the tiny European Scops Owls and others that normally are found in a warm climate, have to have a heat lamp during the cold winter months. If it is really cold, we even put up building plastic on the front of the pen to make it warmer. Running a heat lamp can be pretty expensive. Finding out where an owl would normally be found and about the local climate can be very important when you come to house and care for your bird. There are books that will give you this important information.

Voice

Owls in the wild (**and** in captivity) can be very noisy. Tawny Owls can be heard up to half a mile away when they start serious calling in the spring. You should remember this if you have neighbours living nearby. Of course, as owls generally are nocturnal, most of the calling is at night – and that can be pretty annoying if you are trying to get to sleep.

Owls have all sorts of different calls: the Tawny Owl does the well-known 'Twit Twoo', but it also has a blood-curdling shriek. Snowy Owls grunt like pigs. Eagle Owls hoot in a different pattern from the Tawny Owl, but can also bark like a dog. It is very scary if they do it late at night as you walk past their aviary. I jump out of my skin if I am not expecting it! The Barn Owl is one of the quieter owls, but it can be noisy as well, making a churring noise sometimes described as 'snoring'. All the owls are much noisier in the spring than at any other time of the year **but** (and you have got to watch for these 'buts' as there will be many of them!), to some species the breeding season is not the time we usually think of as spring. My Bengal Eagle Owls laid eggs in October one year, so we had baby Eagle Owls by early December.

Owls in aviaries in your garden may attract wild owls and then the noise increases. The larger owls may not make a noise for the first year until they are properly mature but, once they have learned to hoot, they don't stop! It is a very important factor to think about before having an owl.

I have talked about the calling noises owls make, and they are all very different. They also have warning noises if they don't like things. They will clop their beaks and hiss if they are upset; both noises mean that the owl is not a happy owl. This may mean you should stop whatever you are doing that is upsetting the bird in the first place.

Remember, owls can be very noisy!

Hearing

Owls have superb hearing. A substantial part of their hunting is done by using their directional hearing; as much, if not more so, than their eyesight. An owl's ears are situated in more or less the same place as ours, behind the eyes. Look at the stiff ring of feathers that surround the face, making the edge of what is called the facial disc, and you will find the ears situated under that ring of feathers. In many owls, one of the ears is located a little higher than the other. This is so the owl can pinpoint exactly where its quarry is on the ground as it flies slowly across listening for noises in the long grass. The ear holes can easily be seen when the birds are tiny because their feathers have not yet grown and covered the head.

The owl's ears are located behind the facial disc; the feather ear tufts are not used for hearing.

Sense of smell

Basically, owls don't have a sense of smell, so you can wear whatever scent you like and it won't bother them. Almost all the diurnal birds of prey (eagles, hawks and so on) are the same as owls and have no sense of smell. However there is one that does; the Turkey Vulture has developed a sense of smell so that it can find carcasses hidden in the undergrowth of the rain forests of South America. None of the owls have managed this progress in their evolution.

Eyesight

Owls have good eyesight, but not superb like the day-flying birds of prey, and they appear to have fairly poor close-up vision. When you see older people holding a piece of paper at arm's length away from them to read – well, if owls could read they would do the same thing because they are a little short sighted.

They see mostly in black and white. It's all to do with the make-up of their eye. What they lose in colour vision they make up for by being able to see really well in the dark. Some owls may be able to see some colour but a lot of research is still to be done on the subject.

Their eyes are very large, taking up nearly a third of their skull. The eyes are very vulnerable so, when the owl gets really close to its prey, the last few feet of the hunt is done by hearing and memory as it closes its eyes to protect them. Our trained owls do the same thing when we give them a piece of meat from our fingers, they close their eyes just as they take it, but sometimes they miss and that can be painful!

Don't miss!

'Still hunting': from his vantage point the owl can spot potential prey.

How they hunt

Like all birds of prey, owls use their feet to catch their prey. That is why they have large, powerful feet. They also have powerful beaks and they use their beaks and feet to kill what they have caught. So, don't get bitten and, even more important, don't get grabbed by the foot of an owl – it's painful.

Owls normally hunt in one of two ways. They do a great deal of what is called 'still hunting', that is, they have a number of favourite perches in their territory and they move from one to another. They sit quietly for a time on the chosen perch, listening and watching. If they wait and find nothing, they move to another perch and so on until, hopefully, they find something to eat. A second method, and Barn Owls are often seen hunting like this, is to quarter the ground. The owl flies slowly from side to side, crossing and re-crossing rough pasture or other suitable hunting areas. It flies fairly low so that it can hear what is going on. The whole time it is looking and listening for mice, voles, insects or even frogs and lizards on which to prey.

Taste

Owls do have a sense of taste and, depending on what a young owl has been reared on, it can be quite fussy about its food. Certainly, some creatures in the wild play on this sense of taste. For example, toads have a special sort of poison in their skin so, to an owl, they probably taste awful.

It is a good idea to feed your owl many different types of food so that it doesn't get fussy about what it eats. Not only is having just one food type bad for an owl but if, for example, it only eats mice and suddenly you can't get any, things can become very difficult unless you can persuade your owl to eat something else.

Your owl will not appreciate the poisonous skin of a toad.

Touch

Owls, especially young owls, have such soft feathers that, if you shut your eyes and gently touch one, you won't actually be able to feel straight away when you have reached the outer feathers. Owls have bristle-like feathers around their beaks which are very sensitive. The mother owl touches these when she is feeding her young and the baby owl will feel it and take the food from her beak.

You will often see people stroking birds. In fact, this is a bad thing to do, especially on the head and back. Birds don't much like having a hand put over their head and, if you stroke a bird a great deal, you will take all the waterproofing off its feathers. If you really want to stroke an owl you should very gently stroke its chest but, generally, I would advise against stroking, however tempting it may be. However, it is a good idea to get the owl used to you touching its feet so that it doesn't mind its feet and legs being handled.

11

Cars and lorries are, unfortunately, one of the main killers of owls in this country.

Survival in the wild

Lots of things affect owls in the wild. Many young owls die of starvation. Hunting other animals is much harder than eating grass, for example, so many young and some older owls fail to catch enough to eat and die. Very cold or very wet weather could make hunting hard, very hot weather could make the small animals and insects become scarce, so the owl dies as well. It could be simply that the owl never learns to fend for itself well enough. The on-going changes in farming have caused huge problems for owls, especially the Barn Owl, as the habitat has changed and the owl has failed to adapt.

The other main killer of owls in the United Kingdom, apart from lack of good hunting habitat, is cars and lorries. Many owls are killed on the roads each year. They have not evolved well enough to cope with the increasing amount of traffic on the roads today.

Other causes of death are drowning in water troughs and water butts. Owls hit wire fences, particularly barbed wire and electricity cables. Little Owls are hunted by other birds of prey, including Tawny Owls. Owls do not live as long in the wild as they can in captivity, but then in the wild it is rare for animals and birds to get old. Once they are less fit and strong they will die – this is perfectly natural and leaves space for the younger owls to come along, take over their territories and start to breed, thus continuing the line.

Chapter 2 Knowing about owls

Where to find information

It is really important to find out all about owls before deciding that you want one yourself, and I don't mean by reading only this book. You have to be prepared to do your homework by travelling to see how owls are kept in different situations, talking to people, seeing how they look after their owls, and by reading up about owls in different books.

There is only one problem which is that not all places open to the public are caring for their owls in the right way. The advice given by many people is wrong. Therefore, you have to be very careful. The best way is to listen to a few different people and judge which ones seem to care for their birds best and also talk the most sense – then listen to them and not to the others.

Libraries

Today libraries seem to be forgotten centres of information. Often school children (and students) write to us because they have been given a project and, basically, want us to do it. Well, I have enough to do, thanks! If you go to a local library and ask for a book on a particular subject, the staff should be able to help. If they don't have a book, ask them to get one for you. It is a much better way to learn than to ask someone like me to write the whole thing out for you, which I won't do anyway! Learning how to get information will stand you in very good stead in the future, and it can be exciting to do it for yourself.

Queries

It is very easy to keep asking people questions until you get the answer that **you** want – which may not necessarily be the right one. The main thing you have to remember is that keeping owls is more complicated than keeping more recognised pets. If you want to fly an owl, making a mistake can easily kill your owl. I always say to people that the main difference between training a dog, cat or even a horse compared with training an owl, is that if you make mistakes or don't do the job well with the first three, all you will have is a badly trained animal. If you make a mistake in training any bird of prey, you will probably kill it.

Questions you need to ask

- What sort of owl is the best one to keep, and what do you want it for?
- What sort of aviary must you build for it?
- What sort of food does it eat, where can you obtain the food and how do you store it?
- Have you got a veterinary surgeon who is prepared to look after your owl if it becomes ill?
- Are you able to get to the surgery quickly in an emergency, and have you enough money to pay the vet bills if your bird needs treatment? It might be an idea to insure your bird in case you end up with huge vet bills. My vet bills are about £6,000 a year!

Do your homework before getting an owl. Libraries are good sources of information.

Books

It is a very good idea to get some other books about owls. If you are interested in owls, they will be nice to have anyway, and the more you know about owls in general, the better you will be able to look after one. There is a reading list at the back of this book.

Where to fly your owl

If you are going to fly your owl, you must find somewhere where you have the owner's permission to fly. It is not a good idea to fly an owl in the local park. Can you get to the place where you want to fly? Local farm land is best if you can get permission from the farmer. I was able to fly my birds in a school playing field after everyone had gone home, but that was a long time ago.

Holidays

It is not a good idea to take your owl on holiday with you. You must find someone who is prepared to look after your owl while you are away. This is one of the reasons why you should build a really good aviary, so that it is easy for someone to feed and care for your owl without having to go into the aviary to do it. Tell your vet that you are going away so that, if there is a problem, whoever is caring for your owl can call the vet who will be able to help even though you are not there.

Chapter 3 Housing your owl

Indoors or out?

It is important to remember that your owl needs its own home. Although you can bring it into your house on occasion, owls should not be asked to live in the house with you. To start with, they cannot be house trained and will make a very nasty mess on curtains, carpets and furnishings. They do not understand about windows and can fly into the glass and injure themselves badly Like any animal they need to have their own space, so it is best to build a good aviary outside with all that your owl needs for a comfortable, happy and safe life.

Build well and strongly

Without doubt, the aviary will be the biggest expense of owning an owl. If it is poorly constructed, rain, snow and winter gales could all damage or blow away your aviary and your owl.

Planning permission

The first thing you have to do is to make sure that you have planning permission. Check with the planning department of your local council; they will be able to let you know if you have to obtain permission to put up a decent aviary. It is not a good idea to build an aviary without checking this first, because if someone thinks you should not have built one and complains, the council can make you take it down. You will have to draw out a plan of the aviary to show the planning department.

Size

If you are going to have a medium-sized owl as your first bird, as I would suggest you do, then you will need an aviary about 3m x 3.6m x 2.1m high (10ft x 12ft x 7ft high). This will give plenty of room in which your bird can fly and exercise.

Walls

I have found that owls do better if the aviary has three sides of timber or some other solid material and one side open, covered in weldmesh (**not** chicken wire or chain link). I think that tongue and groove is the best and most attractive timber to use. If you get it tantalized before it arrives it will not have to be treated for many years.

The weldmesh should be ten gauge and 2.5cm x 5cm or 7.6cm (1in x 2in or 3in) mesh. Paint it with black emulsion; this will make it much easier to see through and nicer to look at. All our pens are built on a low brick wall; it keeps the timber off the ground, stops animals putting paws through the wire, looks very nice and makes a good place on which to build the bath.

Roofing

All our pens are built with a completely covered-in roof but, if you prefer some of the roof area to be open, then at least half the pen roof should be covered and the other half made

This completely open-sided aviary was not sturdy enough to withstand winter gales and gave insufficient shelter.

of wire. I prefer to use a roofing material called Onduline. It is a paper and tar material. Unlike tin, steel or plastic, it stays reasonably cool in summer and retains heat in winter. It also prevents condensation dripping on your owl in very cold weather. It is available in various colours and is easy to use. You will need a couple of transparent sheets to ensure that adequate light is let in.

17

Your owl will appreciate having a permanent bath pan in its aviary.

Bath

All owls like to drink and to bath. You can build a bath onto one of the walls, which means that it can be cleaned and filled from the outside. The advantage of this is that anyone can do this without disturbing the owl in the pen. Otherwise the plastic pans that go under the very big flowerpots you can buy from garden centres are quite good. The bath should not be more than about 10–12cm (4–5in) deep and about 45–60cm (18–24in) wide. If you want to be able to get at a pan-type bath from the outside, build a small platform up against the wire. To get at whatever type of bath you choose, build a frame and add a door, a little bigger than the size of the bath. Remember to put the door hinges on the top of the frame, not the bottom or sides, then the door will always swing shut even if you forget to close it properly.

Doors and fixtures

You should **always** have a double door system. That is, you open one door, go into a passage, close the door and only when the outer door is closed do you open the inner door to go into the pen. You have no idea how many people have lost their owl because they had only one door and the owl flew past them out of the door. A passage on the back or side of the pen is best, and also means that the owl is not flying at the wire in an effort to get out whilst you are trying to open the door. Put a good, strong padlock on the outside

door which should keep your owl safe and secure from people who might not have the best of intentions. If you are going away and someone else is going to look after your owl for a few days, put a padlock on the inner door as well. That way, no one can go into the pen unless you have given them the key.

Feed drawer

You should put a feed drawer on the inner passage so that at feeding time you can go into the service passage, open the drawer, drop in the food and close it. In this way you need not go into the pen to feed the owl. This will also make it easier for anyone else who may be feeding your owl for you.

Flooring and perches

Sand on the floor of the pen is easy to keep clean and soaks up the droppings. If you are going to put concrete under the sand, leave some holes for perches to be dropped in. We like to use branches with lots of good perches, dug into the floor so that they look like trees. We also put up ledges on the sides of the pen as young owls like to lie down. A stump or two adds variety as well.

Outside the aviary

It is best not to have grass growing right up to the pen as it will need mowing and the mower can frighten an owl badly. A gravel path right round the aviary is easy to keep clean and tidy and will prevent other animals trying to dig in.

Pricing a pen

Here are all the materials that you will need to build a pen 3m x 3.6m x 2.1m high (10ft x 12ft x 7ft high) with a service passage and a double door system.

Walls and timber for the roof

222 bricks for the base; 3 sheets 9mm sterling board; 130m (428ft) of 7 x 5cm (7 x 5in) timber; 234m (768ft) of tongue and groove cladding.

Roofing materials

Onduline: eight solid sheets; two clear sheets; four ridge pieces.

Wire front

7 x 2.5cm (3 x 1in) ten gauge; weldmesh to cover front.

Hinges, bolts and so on

Cost

At the Centre, we usually reckon that an average size pen costs about £800 to build.

Finally

You must have your aviary finished well before your owl arrives.

Chapter 4 Feeding your owl

What do owls eat?

If you are squeamish about handling dead things, then now is the time to decide that you don't want to keep an owl, because owls eat dead animals and birds and you will have to handle them, cut them up and clear up any unused food each morning.

Where to keep the food

To make sure you always have a good supply of food for your owl, you will need a small deep-freeze in which to keep the stores. I don't think it is a good idea to keep frozen rats, mice and chicks in the same freezer as human food. A small upright freezer means that you will be able to have one month's supply of food ready at all times. You may need a fridge as well, although if you use a plastic container with a well-fitting lid, you can keep some food in the house fridge.

Your deep-freeze must be filled with several types of food before you get your owl.

Different kinds of food

As I said earlier, it is not a good idea to feed any bird just one type of food. Apart from being very boring for the bird, if one type of food becomes unavailable, you can always switch to another. The most commonly-used food is what are called day-old chicks, also known as 'hatchery waste'. It is sad, but some hens are bred solely to lay eggs and, as males don't lay eggs, they are sorted out on the first day they hatch and killed straight away. They are a good source of food but should not be used exclusively. You must give your owl other food as well.

Rats are very good food for the medium and large owls, but a bit tough for the small owls. Mice are very good for the medium and small owls but become expensive if you give them to the larger owls. Sometimes hamsters are available from food suppliers and owls love them. I know that you might be upset about feeding a hamster to your bird, but remember, it will have been dead and frozen long before you get it.

Quail are often used for diurnal birds of prey. They are a little high in protein for owls but are good for them to eat occasionally. Rabbit can be used but has to be cut into smaller chunks for all but the largest owls.

Food that should not be used

Never use anything if you don't know where it came from. For example, you might see a freshly-killed rabbit or pheasant on the road and think it would be good food for your owl – and it might well be. On the other hand, perhaps it was run over because it had been shot and injured or was ill. You can never tell, so it is best not to risk it.

Never use anything that has been shot, either with a shotgun or a rifle, as traces of lead can be left in the body and it is very easy for an owl to get lead poisoning.

Always feed food that is either fresh or freshly thawed out. Do not feed old food, and do not re-freeze food.

If you get in a new load of food for the freezer, make sure that you move the older food to the top and put the new in the bottom. This is called rotating stock, and ensures that you do not feed really old frozen food.

When to feed

We have found that it is best to feed our owls in the evening, unless they are trained and flying birds in which case they get fed when they fly. For a moulting, resting or breeding bird, feeding in the evening means that the owl will feed just after dusk and the food will not have been sitting there all day. This is particularly important in hot weather when the food can go off quickly, and in very cold weather when it can freeze before the owls go down to feed.

Parent owls with babies must be fed at least twice a day

How much to feed

This is one of the most difficult questions I have to answer – so I don't! It depends on many things. Growing baby owls have to have as much food as they like and will probably feed at least twice a day, and up to

Do not consider keeping an owl if you are squeamish.

four times a day when they are really tiny. Trained owls have to have their food regulated because, if they eat too much, they will become 'fed up' and refuse to fly. Full-grown owls do not need as much as young growing owls, but each bird has its own appetite.

When you get your owl, ask the breeder how much it is eating and what sort of food they feed; then follow their recommendations until you understand your owl a bit more. Probably the best way to proceed is to give a certain amount of food and, if all of it is gone in 12 hours, give more next time until, eventually, not all the food is eaten. Then reduce the amount a little.

Owls eat less when the weather is hot and often they eat less if it is raining. If you intend to breed owls then I suggest that you find a good book, as it is a complicated subject and too involved for this book.

See the section on training to see what to feed trained owls.

Pellets

Owls eat things that are pretty indigestible, such as fur, feathers, beatle wings and even bones. They have to get rid of these in some way and so they condense all the indigestible food into a pellet inside their stomach. They then regurgitate or 'cast' the pellet. The pellet is usually lozenge shaped and contains squashed up fur, bones and so on. In fact, dissecting the pellet of wild owls is how scientists discover what they eat in the wild. Most owls will bring up a pellet every day if they are eating indigestible material. Sometimes they can go a couple of days without producing a pellet if they are digesting bones and turning them into calcium for growing bones.

Drinking

Contrary to many people's beliefs, owls do drink and water must be available at all times. The bath should be sufficient if it is cleaned out very regularly, that is, twice a week in winter and every day in summer.

Owls regularly cast pellets.

You could have a smaller bowl in your pen solely for drinking water but it will have to be very stable so that it does not tip over. It is probably a good idea to have it close to a wall with a separate opening door to make it easy to remove, and the bowl should be cleaned and refilled every day.

Bathing

Owls love to bath in hot weather or on a sunny day after many grey days, particularly if you have just cleaned and filled the bath. The bath should be large enough for your owl to flap around easily and get nice and wet, but not so deep that it could drown. The only time to discourage an owl from bathing is in very cold and freezing weather, but then the bath water will probably be frozen anyway, so it won't be able to.

Where to get food

Subscribe to a magazine called the *Falconer's Magazine*. Lots of people advertise food, equipment, birds and so on. Sometimes it contains articles about owls and, at the moment, is the only magazine available about birds of prey.

Chapter 5 Choosing your owl

If you want to breed owls, then it is best to select a species for which you can find good homes for the young. That is the most important criterion for choosing the right species to breed. It is not a good idea to breed Barn Owls or European Eagle Owls at the moment because it is very difficult to find good homes for the young. Otherwise it doesn't really matter except that it is not a good idea to learn about captive breeding by using very expensive or very rare owls. See the reading list for a good book about breeding owls.

I am assuming that at this stage you do not want to get a pair of owls for breeding, but that you want a tame owl that will be reasonably easy to train and to fly.

As I said at the beginning of the book, there are many species of owl but only a few are suitable for handling and flying, and not all would be suitable for a first time owner.

The smaller the owl, the harder it is to train and the easier it is to make a mistake which could result in its death. Even Barn Owls, which are very popular, do not make a good beginner's bird in my opinion. They are small owls so, if their weight drops too far or too quickly they will die and, sadly, many do. If your owl dies, then you are the one responsible for its death, make no mistake about that. It is easy to blame all sorts of things but, when it

The Barn Owl is not an ideal beginner's bird.

comes down to it, you are the one who wanted an owl so the responsibility for its life, its wellbeing and its death is yours and yours alone.

My favourite beginner's owl is the Bengal Eagle Owl, also known as the Indian Eagle Owl, *Bubo bengalensis*. It is not one of the huge Eagle Owls but is a nice size and all the ones that I have known have had really nice temperaments. The Magellan's Eagle Owl, as it is called in the United Kingdom (probably wrongly), is another owl of a similar size. This is a subspecies (close cousin) of the Great Horned Owl but is smaller.

Striped Owls are a reasonable size as well, although not that easy to find. Even Great Grey Owls are a good size for a first-time owner. Although they look huge they don't weigh half as much as some of the really big owls. The problem with Great Greys and some of the other species is that they are still fairly rare in captivity and, therefore, expensive. However, this should change, given time.

The very large species, such as the European Eagle Owl, the Snowy Owl and the Great Horned Owl, are all too large for children and can be difficult to handle unless you are experienced. I suppose what I am saying is that, in my opinion, any medium sized, common species of owl would be suitable, with the Bengal Eagle Owl being the best.

The Bengal Eagle Owl is a good choice for your first owl.

Chapter 6 Getting your owl

Where from?

You have to be careful when deciding where to get your owl. Just as in the dog world, sadly you can buy a bad dog because not all dog breeders care about how they breed dogs; so, in the owl world, there are people who are not as careful as they might be about breeding owls, and you can end up with problems.

The answer is to go to a reputable breeder, specialist zoo or falconry centre that may be breeding the species of owl which you are interested in. I do not recommend getting an owl from either a pet shop or a garden centre. The chances are that they did not breed the owl and therefore know nothing about its history. I am also very un-impressed by people who sell owls without making sure that the buyer has a pen ready, a good food supply and understands a little about how to care for an owl.

If you get your bird from the person who reared it, you should know how it was reared, exactly how old it is, what food it was reared on, how much it is eating, what its parents look like and many other things that are useful to know. You will also require a Captive Breeding Document from the breeder. The owl should have a closed ring on its leg that fits well and is not too small. If the bird is a European species (which a Bengal Owl is not), it will need an Article 10 Certificate which is issued by the government department called the Department of the Environment, Transport and the Regions (DETR).

How should my owl have been reared?

You should never try to train an injured wild owl or a parent-reared owl – they are very wild and it is unfair on the owl to try to train it. In fact, some wild owls and owls that have been parent-reared would rather die than be trained. The best owls for training are hand-reared owls that have been reared in a group of young owls.

I disapprove strongly of people who sell two-week-old owls, particularly to beginners. It is not fair on either the young owl or the person who is buying it. Too many things can go wrong with a baby owl at this stage unless the owner is very experienced. The other problem is that the bird becomes totally imprinted on (obsessed with) the human that reared it. This is all very well when it is a young bird but, when it gets older and wants to breed, not only will it be interested in breeding with the person who reared it, but it may get very aggressive towards other members of the family and even attack them. This is definitely to be avoided.

The best way to rear owls so that they are tame and suitable for training and flying is to hand rear them in a group of young owls. In this way, they will grow up together, play and relate to each other, and should breed naturally in the future. In this way, they should not get too fixated on one person or become aggressive in later life.

Leave your owl with the breeder until it is hopping about the aviary, not quite able to fly but reasonably well feathered. A good breeder should put the young owls where they can see many things and give them plenty of handling. In this way they will stay tame and friendly. It is much the same advice as for choosing a puppy – go to a reputable breeder, don't get an overly young bird and make sure it has been well handled.

Purchase your owl from a reputable source.

Collecting your owl

Build a good travelling box in advance which is the right size for the owl (ask the breeder about dimensions). The box should be dark, with a sliding door at one end, no windows but one-inch air holes all round the top of the sides, and carpet on the floor. Do not put in any perches because a baby owl could fall and hurt itself. Do not put food or water in the box. The baby will not eat and the water will only spill into the box and make the owl wet and miserable. Six hours is the maximum time you should leave the bird in the box at this age unless you are a very experienced bird handler.

Choose a cool day to collect your owl. Never travel your bird on a hot day. Heat kills more quickly than almost anything. Watch out for exhaust fumes as well. Owls are very sensitive to fumes of any sort. Nice fresh air is what they like.

At home

When you arrive home, take the bird out of the box and put it into the aviary. The only time this is not a good idea is if you get a young owl early in the year and the weather is very cold. If this is the case, you should ask the breeder where the babies have been kept at night. If the young owls have been brought in, that is what you should also do.

Don't expect your owl to be cheerful and friendly and feed the first day. It is likely to be scared and upset by the move, so give it time to get used to its new surroundings. If it doesn't feed that day, don't worry, it will probably feed the next with no problems.

Give the young owl time to settle. Go into the pen and let the bird get used to you. And **no stroking**. As I said earlier, most owls tolerate but do not enjoy it

Owls enjoy playing with tennis balls.

and constant stroking quickly ruins the waterproofing on the feathers. Play with its feet and beak, maybe give it a very occasional stroke on the breast, but that is all.

Once your owl has settled and is eating well, you can go in and even take it some toys. Tennis balls are good; they are small enough to be played with but not so small that they can be swallowed. The slight furriness on them is nice for the owl – perhaps it reminds the owl of mice. Crumpled-up newspaper also makes a good toy that your owl will learn to pounce on and tear up – and you will have the fun of clearing the mess up afterwards.

Chapter 7 Training your owl

Which owls to train?

I discussed this in the last chapter. You need a hand-reared baby that has been reared in a group of young owls until it is starting to grow its adult feathers and hopping about the aviary but is not yet flying. A medium-sized species will be the best and means you are less likely to kill it if you make a mistake.

When to start

It is very important not to start training your owl too early. Young owls, like most young things, have soft bones when they are growing and, if you start training too early, you can damage them permanently. You can put the jesses (leather straps) on the owl's legs once it is about seven weeks old, but it is important that you do not hold the owl by those straps until it is fully grown and almost fully feathered.

However, almost as soon as you have got your bird at five weeks or so, you can encourage it to sit on your fist and eat bits of meat from your fingers. Remember, though, the owl must not be able to hurt itself by falling off the gloved hand. Did I tell you that you must buy and wear a good falconry glove? Well you must, or you will get several nasty holes in your hand.

A proper falconry glove is a sound investment.

Equipment

The following list is what you will need for your bird:
- a weighing machine
- a good quality falconry glove
- a canvas bag of some sort in which to keep meat for training
- Aylmeri Jesses with hunting straps and mews straps
- a leash
- a swivel
- bells (optional)
- a training line, called a creanse
- a dummy rabbit or mouse for smaller birds
- a bath, if you have not built one into the pen

The weighing machine is one of the most important pieces of equipment because you have to weigh your owl every day once you start the training sessions. Make sure you buy an accurate model.

Some people will try to sell you old welding gloves and heaven knows what else, but these are cheap and will not stop the owl's talons going through into your hand. Also, they are very thick which means that you cannot hold the jesses properly. Take my advice: buy a properly designed and made falconry glove that is easy to wear, comfortable and in which you can handle your owl with ease.

Your owl will wear leather straps on each leg with a thin piece of leather attached at all times except during rest periods. These straps are called jesses and they will stay on the owl for about nine months every year. Then for three to four months you need to give your owl a break from flying so that it can have a rest, moult out its old feathers and grow new ones. During that time you should cut off the old jesses or they will get very hard. When your owl has finished moulting and is looking really smart, you will have to put on brand-new, soft jesses with new hunting straps ready to start training again.

To keep the jesses soft during the flying period you should grease them every other day with a leather preparation. We buy a product which can be purchased from most saddlers' shops. It is red and very sticky, so care must be taken not to get any on the owl's feathers.

Your owl will not need to wear a swivel and leash as it will not be tethered. However, if you are going to carry it around outside the pen, it is a good idea to put on the leash and swivel so, if the owl gets upset, you are less likely to let it go by mistake. **Never** leave the leash and swivel on when the owl is in the pen or it may get caught up and die. **Never** fly the bird with the leash and swivel on or it may get hung up in a tree and die.

Birds should only be flown with the leather anklets, or bracelets as they are sometimes called, and the thin hunting straps attached, and nothing else except perhaps a bell unless you are rich enough to buy a telemetry set (used for tracking animals).

Training

Once your owl has settled in the pen and is feeding and growing well, you can start the initial training. By this stage, your owl should be nearly full grown and on one feed per day in the evenings. All you do is go in at feeding time and whistle every time you give your owl a piece of food. It will quickly start to associate the whistle with the food. Then try sitting a little way off in the pen and whistling, and see if your owl will walk, run or hop over to you – if it does then you have succeeded in starting the training. You can even take it out into the garden before it can fly and do the same thing outside. Always make sure that there is nothing about that could hurt your young owl, such as a dog or large cat.

Continue to do this every day. Don't reduce the bird's weight at this stage – that doesn't happen until the bird is full grown and flying well around the pen.

Once your owl starts to flap up to the perches in the pen, continue to whistle but now encourage it to fly or hop to your fist. Even a tiny hop is a step in the right direction. You should encourage your owl to stay on the fist, even to be carried around the aviary.

Every time you call a bird to the fist, reward it with a piece of meat about the size of a new one pence piece. The owl's appetite will lessen as it feeds so it will respond to your calling more slowly. You don't want this to happen, so I suggest that you limit the number of times you call the bird to the fist to about 4–6 times each day and no more, until it is flying loose and knows what you want of it.

You should weigh your owl every day before flying to see at what weight it behaves best. This is really important because, unless you know this, you will not know why your bird behaves, or misbehaves. Write down the weight in a notebook every day, together with how the bird performed in the training session and what the weather was like. This information will help you in the future.

Weight of trained birds

This is a difficult subject because a bird will not behave at the same weight all the time. We find that when it is hot we have to bring down the bird's weight a little more than during cold weather. As the owl gets older it will put on weight and have to be flown at a higher weight. If you take it to a new area to fly, you may have to reduce its weight for the first couple of times. Once it starts to get fit, it will need extra food to turn into muscle. So you can see that one weight will not do for all the bird's life. You have to keep experimenting, putting up the weight if the bird is doing really well and reducing it a little if it is not behaving.

Next steps in training

The next step is taken outside the pen. This has to be done on a training line called a creanse. You will need a good perch for the owl to start from – a post in the ground or an A-frame perch are good. Weigh your owl as usual, attach the swivel and training line and try to call it to the fist as you have been doing in the pen. The chances are that it will ignore you completely the first day as this is something new to it. If it spends the whole time looking round and ignoring you, then no food that day, back in the pen and you should find that it responds better the next day.

Weigh your owl every day and always note down the weight and behaviour.

Each day, take out your owl, put it on the training perch with the training line safely attached to the swivel or mews jesses and try calling it to the fist or the perch. Reward the owl each time it responds with a piece of meat. Always stand holding your fist well away from your body so the owl has plenty of room to land. Increase the distance a little each day. Make sure the bird cannot fly over the top of your fist and get caught up in a tree or over the garden fence.

Space to fly your owl

If you have a very large garden with lots of room you can complete the whole training - even to flying free - in your own garden. If you have got only a small garden, you will have to take your bird somewhere else to fly it once you reach the stage of longer flights. I talked about where to fly in Chapter 2; it must be somewhere safe away from people who might frighten your owl or, conversely, might be frightened of your owl. It must be away from roads so the owl does not fly across and get run over. It must be away from all dogs that you do not know personally and that you can guarantee are safe with a flying owl. Always make sure you have permission to fly on any land you think might be suitable. As I said before, it is a good idea to sort out your flying areas before you get your owl.

Continue the training, either in your garden or your chosen area. Eventually, your owl

Choose a safe place, away from cats and dogs, to fly your owl.

should fly to your fist or to a perch where you have put a piece of meat up to about 45m (50yds) away. Each time you call your owl, whistle and wave the meat about in your bare hand to get the owl's attention before you put it on your gloved fist or the perch.

When the owl is flying to you or the perch regularly with no hesitation, then it is ready to have the training line and mews jesses and swivel taken off and be flown free!

Flying free

Choose a day when you and your family have plenty of spare time, a day when the weather is good and not windy. Behave in exactly the same way you have all through the training. First pick up and weigh your owl, then take it to the flying ground. Place it on its normal perch and call it to the fist in the usual way. Don't change anything on the first few days of flying free.

Once you, your family and your owl are confident, try different perches to call from and to. Place the owl on the low branch of a tree and call it from there. Do all sorts of different things so that it gets used to change. If you find something that it does not like, either avoid it or reduce the owl's weight a little and work on that thing until the owl is used to it.

You can now introduce the dummy rabbit or mouse. Tie a piece of meat to it and pull it slowly in front of the owl to see if the owl will chase it. This always takes ages with an owl, so persevere and you should succeed in the end.

During training, you should really try to train and fly it every day or it will forget what you are trying to teach it. Once it is flying free, it will not matter if you miss the occasional day. Because you are keeping it in a good, large pen, it can move around and exercise itself on the days when you are not able to fly it.

When not to fly your owl

It is not a good idea to try to fly your bird when the weather is wet or very windy, as the owl will probably sit in a tree and refuse to move until it has stopped raining and the owl has dried off. On windy days, an owl can literally be blown away, or blown into things and get hurt. Very hot days can be a problem, too, so fly your owl in the evening when it has cooled down.

You may find that one day your owl does not seem keen to come to you and is over weight. That is the whole point of the weighing machine; to let you know when your bird is the wrong weight. Don't fly your bird that day.

Do not fly your owl on windy days or he may, literally, be blown away from you.

Chapter 8 Travelling your owl

We talked about travelling in Chapter 6. It is very important to remember that hot weather can easily kill owls in pens and boxes so, unless the journey is absolutely vital, it is much better to leave your owl safely at home in its pen during very hot weather.

If you do not have a flying ground near your home you will have to travel your owl to reach the area where you fly. Do not have the owl loose in your car – this is dangerous and also illegal. You must have a purpose-built box for the owl to travel in; if you aren't good at carpentry, then you must get someone to build a box for you.

The travelling/carrying box

Cardboard boxes do not last, are difficult to open and to carry, and really are no use except in the early stages when you might want to have one in which to carry your young owl about.

Without doubt, the best type of travelling box is a dark box with a sliding door at one end. It needs to be long enough for the owl to sit on the carpeted floor and not touch the ends with its head or tail. Of course, this depends on the size of owl you are going to get. Ask the breeder how long the owl is going to be when it is full grown and build the box a little longer. The box should be high enough so that the owl can stand up at full height and not touch the top. We do not put perches in for our young owls, but a full grown, trained owl might like one. The perch must be high enough off the bottom of the box for the bird's tail not to touch or the feathers will get damaged. The box should be wide enough not to touch the owl's shoulders but not so wide that the owl can open its wings. Most of our boxes are about 60cm long x 50cm high x 40cm wide (24in long x 20in high x 16in wide).

Put carpet on the floor so that the bird cannot slip. Newspaper can be used if the bird is full grown and used to sitting on a perch fixed into the box, but otherwise you must have a fixed, non-slip surface and carpet is the best.

If you are putting in a perch, use a piece of 5cm x 5cm (2in x 2in) timber and fix carpet so that it is comfortable for the owl to sit on and easy for it to grip during the journey.

Drill air holes all around the sides of the box and fix a small bolt to the door so that it does not come open.

If you are only a very short distance from the flying ground, you could walk and carry your owl on your fist, but this is not a good idea if you are going to walk through heavily populated areas. Your owl might become agitated and try to fly off your fist, and people who do not understand will become really upset and cross with you because they will think you are being cruel. It is much better to keep away from crowds, towns and even villages, unless they are very quiet; you will not get any complaints from people and life is much easier.

If you have to travel your bird to the vet, use your normal travelling box. Attend to the box regularly to keep it clean and tidy.

Chapter 9 Your owl and other pets

The smaller the owl, the more vulnerable it is to receiving an injury from another creature. However, having said this, I assume that you will not be getting a small owl because this is not a good idea. Remember that even the largest of owls would not be safe from large dogs and I have heard of Eagle Owls being killed by foxes as well.

Dogs

Any dog that is not well trained and brought up with owls is a potential danger, with the possible exception of tiny dogs such as Yorkshire Terriers and very big owls such as the large Eagle Owls. Other than those exceptions, a loose owl, or even one on your fist, can be attacked by a dog and injured or killed. Never trust any dog unless you know it personally. We do not let any dogs into the Centre except our own and they are fully trained to be safe with all our birds.

I never take my young Labrador pups out onto the flying ground when the larger owls or eagles are flying. To them, a six-week-old pup is a small black rabbit with short ears, and it is asking for trouble. My adult Labradors wander round all the birds, even when they are flying. The dogs are fully trained and would not dream of hurting the birds, and the birds are familiar with the dogs' presence and do not notice them.

Cats

Cats can kill any owl up to the size of a Barn Owl. Large cats can kill bigger owls; cats in pairs are even more dangerous. Any tethered bird (which, of course, you are not going to do to your bird) is particularly vulnerable to cats. One of the problems with a pen with a wire rather than solid roof is that cats will walk on wire roofs at night. This can badly scare the medium and smaller owls, which is why a solid roof would be better.

On the other side of the coin, the large owls can attack cats. Tamed, trained owls are less frightened of cats so are more likely to have a go. For example, my Great Grey Owl, called Bollinger, hates all my cats and, if they come down to the field when he is flying, he will pounce on them. He has small feet so he is unlikely to do them any harm other than scaring them (which is no bad thing if it teaches them to be frightened of owls). However if Blotto, one of my European Eagle Owls, had tried to grab the cats when he was flying I would have had to stop flying him. He is powerful enough to do them some damage, or even kill a small cat if he grabbed it in the wrong place. Luckily, he takes no notice of them or the dogs.

Please don't get me wrong here. I am very against people who over-dramatise birds of prey, calling them red in tooth and claw and liable to attack and kill all sorts of huge animals. Throughout the world, almost all owls rely on mice and voles as the main part of their diet (or insects in the case of the tiny species such as Pearl Spotted Owlets). Even the large owls will spend a great deal more time eating these small mammals than going out and catching larger quarry such as hares. No hunting animal can afford to be injured by its prey; a large brown hare can weigh twice as much as the largest Eagle Owl and is a very strong animal. Anyone who has tried to hold a cat that does not want to be held will know how difficult it is, and people are stronger than owls.

Check for potential dangers before flying your owl.

Other potential dangers

Foxes and badgers

These mammals might try to dig into pens that are not well built. They are capable of killing or injuring all but the largest of the owls. A fox came into the Centre one year and killed three Short-eared Owls through the roof of the pen; another pulled the leg off an Eagle Owl through the wire. This is one of the reasons why you should build a decent aviary and not be content with a cheap, badly-designed one.

Ferrets, stoats, weasels and, worst of all, mink

All these animals can get through gaps into pens that are not well built and can kill all but the largest owls. You should make sure that your pen is built strongly enough so that no other birds or mammals can get in and your owl can't get out.

Ferrets and rats may attack owls, particularly if the owl is small.

Rats
Although the larger owls eat rats, the smaller ones could be injured or even killed by persistent, large rats. Baby owls in the nest are particularly vulnerable to attack. You would be amazed at where a rat can get in, if it really wants to.

Other birds
Although owls are not liable to be killed by other birds (except for large birds of prey and other owls), they can be hassled and frightened by birds such as magpies, crows and even mistle thrushes. If wild bird droppings can fall into the pen from outside, the owls are vulnerable to disease.

Animals that might be frightened by owls
To other animals, such as small cage birds (budgerigars, canaries, finches), hens, pheasants, quail, pigeons, rabbits, guinea pigs, mice and so on, an owl is a major enemy to be feared. Remember that when you site your pen. It would be cruel to your other pets if they could see one of their worst natural enemies living right on top of them day after day. If you do have other livestock, keep it away from where your owl will live and fly.

Having said that, if you want your bird to stay tame and used to you, it should not be in a pen tucked away out of sight of you, your house and everything that is going on.

Household pets may be intimidated by your owl.

Chapter 10 Health care

Owls are pretty tough as long as you are careful and look after them to the best of your ability. If they have a good sized aviary, are kept clean and tidy, have a fresh and varied diet and fresh, clean water you should not have too many problems.

However, you do need to care for your owl very well and keep an eye on it and what it is doing every day. The problem with owls is that they tend to be fairly sedentary during the day, so you really need to watch their behaviour in the early morning or evening to see how they are behaving.

Here are some things for you to watch out for:
- Is your owl eating all right?
- Is it looking well, or sitting hunched up and looking miserable?
- Is it alert and bright?
- Is it flying well, either in the pen or out in your flying ground?
- Are the feathers around the under-tail area clean?
- Is it casting up pellets all right?
- Is it favouring one leg more than the other?
- Does it generally not look right?
- Have you got a gut feeling that all is not well?

If any of the above is worrying you, ring the veterinary surgeon and ask if you should be worried. Always explain the symptoms clearly and, even if it is something that you do not think is important, tell the vet anyway as it is surprising how much the little things matter.

Parasites

Owls can get external and internal parasites. Externally (on the outside) they can get feather mites which eat away at the feathers and ruin them, especially on the back of the neck. They can get what are called 'flat flies', which are horrid. They look a bit like a flattened house fly and are extremely difficult to kill. You can't swat them like a fly; they have to be severely squashed. There are other external parasites, such as ticks, and a bug called scaly mite that attacks the owl's feet and makes them all scaly until, eventually, the toes drop off.

The best way to cope with all these is to treat your owl twice a year with a specially formulated preparation. These change as research improves, so go to your vet and find out what is the best preparation available at the time.

The same can be said for internal parasites such as worms; treat the bird regularly, under instruction from your vet, and everything should be fine.

Diarrhoea

This is a difficult one with owls as about every third dropping is brown, runny and very smelly. If you find that all the droppings are like this, instead of white with black bits in them, you may have a problem. There is a very good preparation called Forgastrin which is very useful to have in the medicine cupboard. Sprinkle it on the food, and it will quickly help the bird's tummy. If the diarrhoea persists, then you should take the owl to the vet as soon as possible.

Coccidiosis

This is another of those parasites, and it affects the bird's intestines. The first sign is that the bird looks generally off colour. If you see any blood in the droppings (these are also called mutes), you must take the owl to the vet very quickly so that it can be treated.

Bumble foot

If your owl gets a swollen foot this could be a disease called bumble foot. It is an infection of the ball of the foot, or sometimes the toes. It is usually caused by poor perches in the aviary, or by the talons being too long and puncturing the foot. The owl should be taken to the vet where a sample will be taken from the swelling to find out which bacteria are involved and then the owl can be treated. Keep flying the bird during treatment as this improves the circulation and the foot will recover more quickly.

Forgastrin is a good cure for diarrhoea.

Overgrown talons and beak

Just like other animals, owls are all different. Some will never get an overgrown beak, others will. It could be due to luck or to what they are eating. If they have food such as rabbit or rat, they have to pull at them rather than eat them whole, and this helps to wear down the beak. If the beak does get overgrown, it will have to be cut back. Unless you are experienced in doing this, it is probably better to ask someone else to do it. Your vet should be able to do it.

If you let the problem go on, the situation will get worse not better, and a badly overgrown beak can stop the owl from feeding properly and eventually it will die.

Cuts and wounds

Unless you have a problem with your pen or your owl hits something when it is flying, cuts and bruises on birds are rare. If your bird gets a minor cut, clean it up and sprinkle on some wound powder which you can get from the vet. A trip to the vet is called for if the injury is more severe.

Broken limbs

If your owl is unable to stand up or fly, there may be something seriously wrong, such as a broken wing or leg. These days, this type of injury can be repaired, but the bird will have to go to an experienced vet who will anaesthetise and X-ray it before fixing any breaks.

Broken limbs should be attended to by your vet.

Regular health check

It is probably a good idea to ask the vet to check over your bird at least once a year, perhaps after the moult, just to make sure that all is well. You will be catching the owl to put on its new jesses, so pop it in its travelling box, take it to the vet for a 'once over' and its yearly worming at the same time.

Hygiene and aviary cleaning

To keep your owl healthy and well, and the aviary attractive and smelling sweet, you need to clean it out regularly. If you have put your perches in the right place, the walls should keep fairly clean. So each week all you have to do is go in and rake up all the droppings and bits and pieces from the sand. If you do this when your owl is a baby, it will get used to the rake and not be worried by the procedure. Sieve the sand, put the rubbish on the fire or compost heap, and put the clean sand back in the pen. Scrub out the bath once a week. A feed drawer, if you put one in, will also need regular cleaning.

Once a year, go into the pen, pick up your owl and put it in its travelling box. Then scrub the pen from top to bottom, cleaning the walls, the perches, the nest ledge, the bath and the feed tray – in fact, everything – with warm water and a suitable disinfectant that you can get from the vet.

Let the pen dry out and then return your owl into its clean, disinfected home. I don't suppose the owl will appreciate the cleanliness, but you will, and it is definitely good for keeping your bird healthy.

End note

If you do decide to have an owl of your own, remember that it is quite a responsibility. It will live a long time if you care for it well. It will need to be housed and fed for many years, and flown if you have trained it.

Owls live longer than most dogs and are probably more time consuming. There is no equivalent of boarding kennels where you can leave them if you go away. Experienced owl veterinary surgeons are not easy to find, and the treatment for a sick owl is often very expensive.

You really need to think about having an owl and all it entails before you get one. During one period, from Christmas to Easter, I was asked to find homes for at least 15 Eagle Owls of various species and several Barn Owls; all because people did not understand how much effort they take to look after. And how noisy they are, as well!

Owls are beautiful birds but are not as easy to train as a Labrador, nor as friendly. You have to know what you are doing or you will make mistakes. An owl that gets lost will probably be a dead owl pretty quickly.

Go to some Bird of Prey Centres and talk to the people who run them. Read some more books about owls and think very hard before asking for an owl to share your life.

My owl's record

Name

Species

Breeder

Date of Birth

Favourite Food

Favourite Toy

Name and Address of Veterinary Surgeon

Telephone Number

Visits to the Vet

Date	Problem	Treatment
Date	Problem	Treatment
Date	Problem	Treatment

Date of First Moult

Bibliography

Allan W Eckert. The Owls of North America. Doubleday and Co. New York.

Heimo Mikkola. Owls of Europe. T & A D Poyser. Calton.

D S Bunn. A B Warburton. R D S Wilson. The Barn Owl. T & A D Poyser. Calton.

Varying Authors. The Birds of North America (the varying American Owls, published in species papers). The Academy of Natural Sciences of Philadelphia.

John Burton. Owls of the World. Peter Lowe. Eirobook Limited.

Krystyna Weinstein. The Owl in art, myth and legend. Grange Books published by Universal Books. London.

Paul A Johnsgard. North American Owls. Smithsonian Institution Press. Washington and London.

John Sparks and Tony Soper. Owls. David and Charles. Newton Abbot.

R Hume. Owls of the World. Dragonsworld Book. Limpsfield. London.

J Parry-Jones. Understanding Owls. David and Charles. Newton Abbot.

J Parry-Jones. Eyewitness Eagle. Dorling Kindersley. London.

J Parry-Jones. Training Birds of Prey. David and Charles. Newton Abbot.

Index